T0380889

Relationship

Morality

Love

Compassion

Truth

Gratitude

Set

Karma

Motivation

Laughter

A Cup of Motivation

Unconventional Wisdom

A Book of Quotes, Words of Wisdom, Memes & Jokes

HOWARD LEE COLE JR

Copyright © 2019 by Howard Lee Cole Jr. 791033
Library of Congress Control Number: 2019900536

ISBN: Softcover   978-1-7960-1092-3
         Hardcover   978-1-7960-1093-0
         EBook   978-1-7960-1091-6

To order additional copies of this book, contact:
Xlibris
1-888-795-4274
www.Xlibris.com
Orders@Xlibris.com

A Cup of Motivation

Unconventional Wisdom

A Book of Quotes, Words of Wisdom, Memes & Jokes

HOWARD LEE COLE JR

"Ignite Your Passion -- Achieve Your Dream"
Mind your thoughts; they turn into words.
Mind your words; they turn into actions.
Mind your actions; they turn into habits.
Mind your habits; they turn into character.
Mind your character; it will become your future!

~Howard Cole~

DEDICATIONS

This book is dedicated to my mother, **Eva Mae Cole** and my father, **Howard Lee Cole Sr.** who are no longer with me. It is also, dedicated to my beautiful wife **Shontà Jones Cole** and my son **Howard Lee Cole III**. I would like to thank every family member and friend in my life who has motivated me and inspired me. It is because of you, I have stepped out of my comfort zone and put this book together.

SPECIAL THANKS TO:

I would like to commend my publishing consultant *Kat Rios* for her efforts on my manuscript. I really appreciate your attention to detail and relentless determination to release a quality product on time. I am proud to have had you as my guide through this long and tedious process. I look forward to working with you again on my volume II book project.
(AKA) Goodtime Howie

Special thanks go out to the Senior Publishing Consultant Supervisor *Sid Wilson* and his team for the wonderful job they did on my manuscript. I was delighted with all your presentation and especially appreciated your suggested programs. The extra time and effort you put in was certainly worthwhile. It was a joy for me to work with such a dedicated and talented team.

To *John Baty*:

Thank you for sharing your work with not only me but the world. Being an artist is often a vulnerable path. You make something so deeply personal and then present it to the world with an open heart. Not everyone is so fearless. If anyone is looking for an artist, please reach out to John Baty at the information below. You can usually find John on the Venice Boardwalk in California.

Email: Baty113@gmail.com Cell Phone: 323-317-3167

TABLE OF CONTENTS

That First Sip

In this first volume, I wanted to share a collection of Quotes, Words of Wisdom, Memes and Jokes that I think are interesting, funny and useful in my life. Some of them are educational, emotional, hard core, edgy and funny. I figured by sharing, I can help somebody through a rough day by putting all these things in one place to revisit from time to time. So, like that first cup of freshly brewed morning cup of coffee, I hope this collection of Quotes, Words of Wisdom, Memes and Jokes make you feel all warm inside.

WHEN THE FIRST SIP OF COFFEE IN THE MORNING TOUCHES YOUR SOUL

Caffeine for your soul!

(Words of Wisdom)

"Still"

Sometimes people around you are being too selfish.
Still love them.
Sometimes if you do good deeds, people will allege it just for show
Still do good.
Sometimes when you are happy, not everyone will be happy for you.
Still be happy.
Sometimes being truthful makes you powerless.
Still be truthful.
Sometimes morality and bluntness make you susceptible
Still be moral and blunt.
Sometimes people are angry when you help.
Still help.
Sometimes life is a gamble.
Still take risk.
Sometimes when you give people your best shot, they cannot always see it
Still give it your best shot

~Howard Cole~

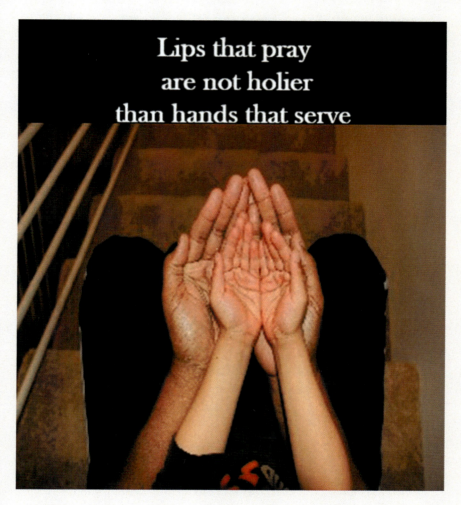

Question: *What are your thoughts about this quote? How do you serve your community?*

"All that you hear
is just an opinion, not a fact.
All that you see
is a perspective, not the truth."

~Howard Cole~

Question: How do you solve your differences?

If you want to "Understand" any difficulty "in America, you
need only to concentrate on "who" benefits from that problem, not who grieves from the problem.

There's always a little honesty behind each "just joking," a little know-how behind each "I don't know," a little passion behind each "I don't mind," and a little pain behind each "I don't care

~Howard Cole ~

Question: What does transparency mean to you?

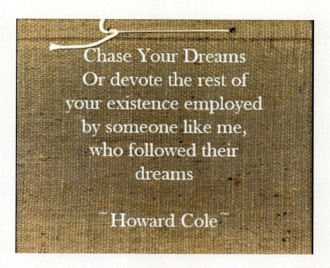

Chase Your Dreams
Or devote the rest of
your existence employed
by someone like me,
who followed their
dreams

~Howard Cole~

Question: What is stopping you from following your dreams? What's your excuse today?

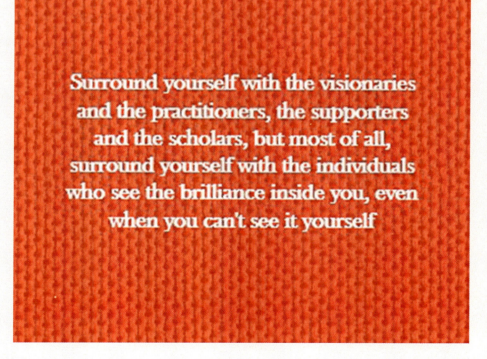

Surround yourself with the visionaries
and the practitioners, the supporters
and the scholars, but most of all,
surround yourself with the individuals
who see the brilliance inside you, even
when you can't see it yourself

Question: What type of people do you surround yourself with? Do you have a mentor?

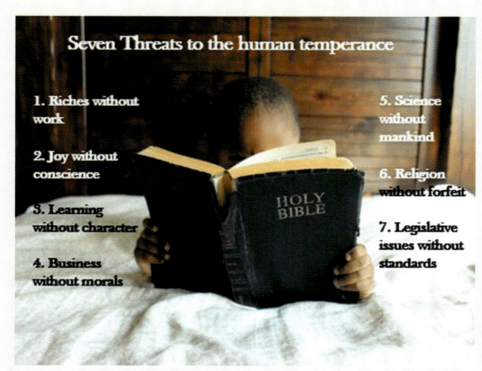

Question: Which one of these seven morality/virtues do you most identify with in your life today? Why?

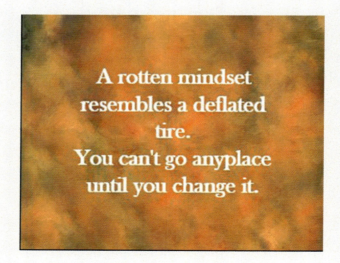

Question: What type of thoughts guide you?

An analyst strolled around a room while explaining anxiety management to a crowd of executives. As he raised a glass of water, everybody expected they'd be asked the "half... filled or half unfilled " question. Rather, with a grin all over his face, he asked: "How big is this glass of water?"

Answers shouted out went from 8 oz. to 16 oz.

He responded, "The total weight doesn't make a difference. It relies upon the length of time I hold it up. On the off chance that I hold it for a moment, it is not a big issue. On the off chance that I hold it for 60 minutes, I'll have a throb in my arm. If I hold it for an entire day, my arm will feel numb and deadened. For each situation, the heaviness of the glass doesn't change, yet the more I hold it, the heavier it moves toward becoming an issue." He proceeded with, "The anxieties and stresses in life resemble that glass of water. Consider them for some time and nothing occurs. Consider them somewhat more and they start to hurt. Furthermore, if you consider them throughout the day, you will feel deadened – unequipped for doing anything."

It's imperative to make sure you relinquish your burdens. As early in the day as you can, put every one of your weights down. Try not to hold them into the night. Make sure to put the glass down!

Question: What does it take for you to put your glass down?

A poor dad that invests time with his kid is superior to a rich dad that just sends checks

Question: What was important to you as a child?

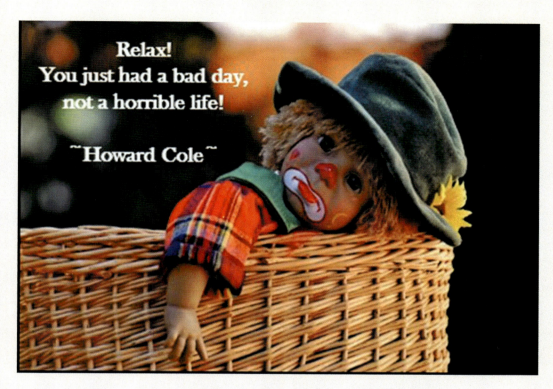

Question: How do you respond to challenges?

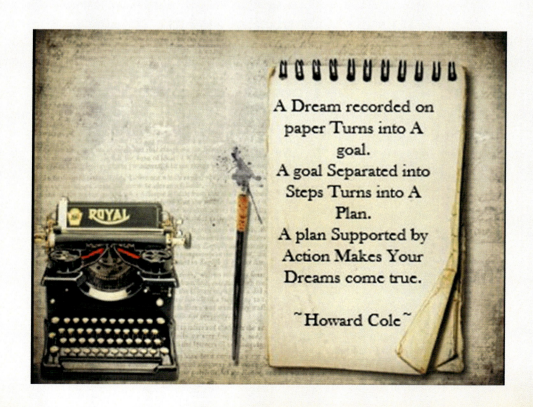

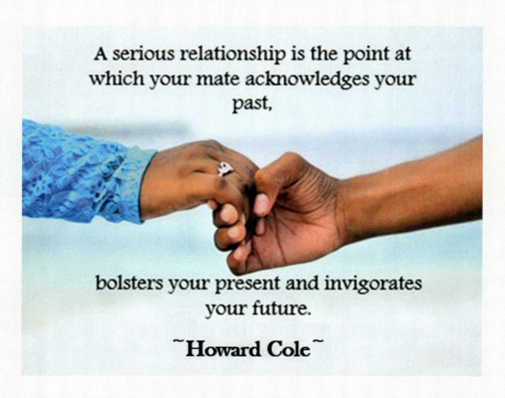

A serious relationship is the point at which your mate acknowledges your past,

bolsters your present and invigorates your future.

~Howard Cole~

I dedicate this page to my wonderful wife Shontà "Jones" Cole who embodies all these qualities in our marriage. My life is such a joy with you in it!!

Question: What does it mean to take responsibility for your actions?

There's a problem with your integrity if "OPPORTUNITY" CONTROLS YOUR Faithfulness.

Question: What drives or dictates your character?

Individuals who are envious of you
don't even understand you don't have everything in perfect order.
They are envious of a battle surrounded by strength.

~Howard Cole~

"Slip-ups are a part of being human.
Value your errors for what they are: valuable life experiences that
can only be learned in the most difficult way possible.
Except if it's a deadly error, which, at any rate, others can gain from."

~Howard Cole~

Question: What was your biggest mistake in life that taught you the best life lesson?

Be candid, but be thoughtful...
Be pleasant, however not naive....
Be clever, but not a smartass....
Be firm, yet respectful...
Be revering and be earnest...

~Howard Cole~

Question: Who is that person in the room that chooses to fight every battle, no matter how big or small? It's okay to use a mirror for this question.

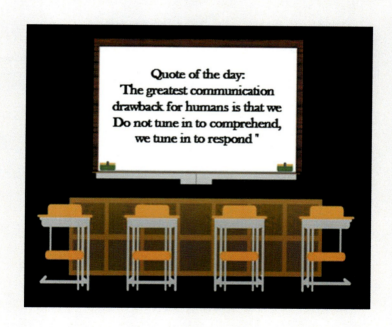

Question: How does this resonate for you?

People will see the adjustment in your demeanor towards them; yet will not see their very own conduct that swayed you to change.

~Howard Cole~

Maturity is difficult. Change is difficult.
However, nothing is as difficult as remaining trapped in the same place you were the year before.

~Howard Cole~

Question: What impactful changes have you made this year?

Question: What trials and tribulation have you gone through in your life that made you a better person?

Don't Be frightened to fail. Be frightened to be in the identical place in 2019 as you were in 2018.

2018 2019

"It's interesting we asked God to transform our circumstances, not realizing he places us in certain circumstances to transform us"

Question: Is it better to remove a situation or endure a situation? Why?

"The most frequent way
Human beings relinquish their influence
Is by assuming they have none"

~Howard Cole~

Question: Describe a time you relinquished something in your life because you didn't know any better?

Individuals who will jeopardize going too far,
Are the only people
Who will ever realize how far they can go."

~Howard Cole~

You should be more bothered by your INTEGRITY
Than with your STATUS.
Your INTEGRITY is the thing you
REALLY ARE while your STATUS is simply what others
THINK you are.

~Howard Cole~

No Cream, No Sugar

(The Keep it Real Side)

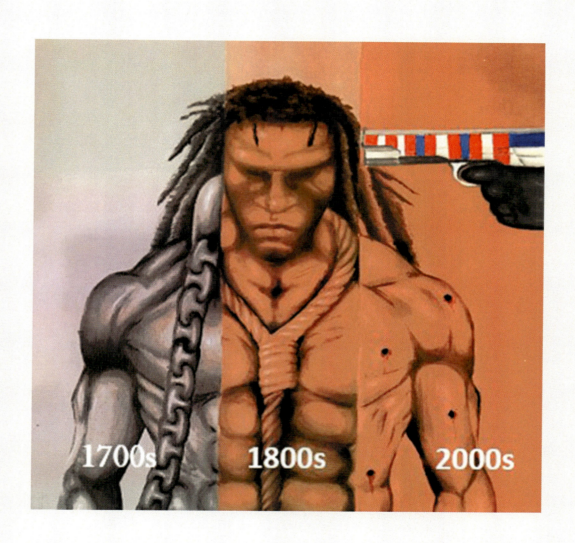

I think females are stupid to dare say they are equivalent to men. They are far greater than men and always have been. Anything you give a female, she will make more significant. On the off chance that you give her sperm, she will give you a child. If you give her a residence, she will give you a home. On the off chance that you give her food, she will prepare you dinner. If you give her a loving smile, she will give you her heart. Females increase and expand what is provided to her. So, on the off chance that you give her any shit, be prepared to receive a heap of Shit.

~Howard Cole~

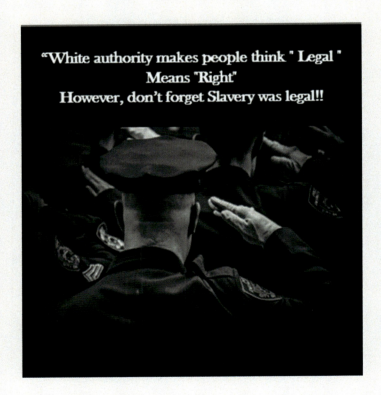

What you tolerate is what you wind up with.
You get exactly what you're settling for.

~Howard Cole~

Try not to kill individuals with Kindness,
On the grounds that not every person merits your generosity.
Kill individuals with silence, because not every person merits your attention.

~Howard Cole~

"I dread the day that innovation will exceed our human Communication.
The world will have a generation of imbeciles"

~Howard Cole~

"Before you determine yourself to have despair or low confidence,
first ensure that you are not, indeed,
simply involved with a bunch of assoles."

~HowardCole~

Most crisis in our lives don't simply enter our lives.
Repeatedly, we generate that crisis,
We either welcome that crisis,
Or we habitually associate with it.

~Howard Cole~

A man that can't be controlled by sex intimidates a female... Because then she needs to bring something substantial to the table.

~Howard Cole~

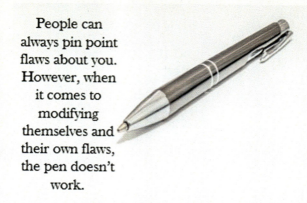

People can always pin point flaws about you. However, when it comes to modifying themselves and their own flaws, the pen doesn't work.

I either give too many fucks about things or I don't give ample enough fucks. I can't seem to establish a center ground for moderate fuck distribution!

~Howard Cole~

Jealous individuals love to jump at the chance to bring up your history. Especially when your current life seems to be superior to theirs

~Howard Cole~

Every now and then you need to abandon people. Not because you couldn't care less, but rather because they don't.

~Howard Cole~

People who are givers need to establish boundaries because takers don't establish any.

~Howard Cole~

Take a plate and toss it on the ground

- alright, done

Did it break?

- Yes

Now say I apologize to it

- I apologize.

Did it return to the way it was previously?

- No

Do you get it now?

~Howard Cole~

"Having a kind heart simply lures beggars, Liars, leeches, users, takers, the inconsiderate, and the unappreciative!"

~Howard Cole~

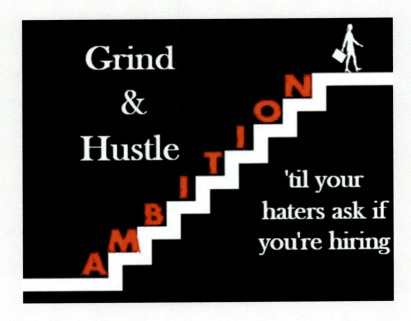

I don't hold Grudges. We cool playa. You might never hear from me again, until the casket drop, but we cool.

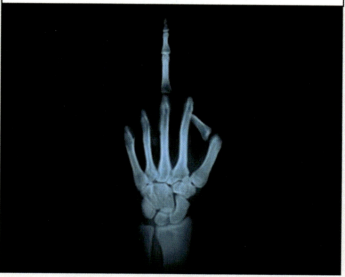

If you
only say
your prayers
when you're
in trouble...
You're in trouble!

I gave you $10, he gave you $20.

You liked him better because he gave you more.

How would you feel if you knew he had $200? And I only had $10.

~Howard Cole~

For you to offend me, I must initially value your fucking opinion!

~Howard Cole~

"If aggression and hostility is inappropriate in America, Aggression and hostility is inappropriate abroad. if it unfitting to be inappropriate protecting black females and black kids and black infants and black males, then it is inappropriate for America to recruit us and make us hostile Abroad in defense of her. And if it is acceptable for America to recruit us and educate us how to be hostile and vicious in defense of her. Then it is acceptable for you and me to do everything in our power to defend our own people right here in this nation.

Here's something to consider Black People.

Why is black fatality so trendy?

Why is it fashionable for us to rap about murdering each other?

I get it. It's simply

entertainment, right?

But if that's the reason, why can't I rap about murdering white individuals in a song?

Why can't I rap about murdering Jews, French people, police, gay

people, elected official, and it be viewed as just entertainment?

Some of you probably winced simply reading that last line.

However, if it was simply entertainment, why does it make a difference?

Who made black fatalities the cool thing to praise?

Who made it cool for us to rejoice in our own devastation?

~Howard Cole~

I am too old for pointless relationships, artificial

exchanges or meaningless conversations.

~Howard Cole~

Don't go bankrupt attempting

to validate you're not broke

to people who are already broke

~Howard Cole~

If your ass owes me money, I prefer you don't live your best life
in front of me on Facebook. That's how shit starts!
Run me my money FOOL!

~Howard Cole~

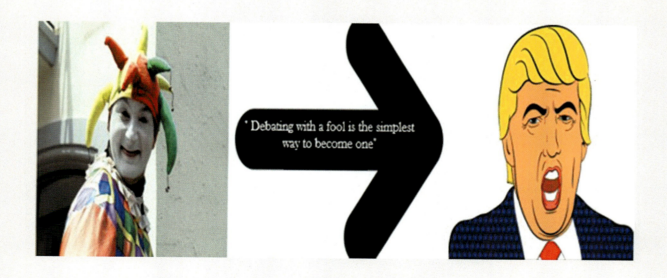

My Old Homies Don't
Recognize the New Me And
My New Homies don't
Understand My History

~Howard Cole~

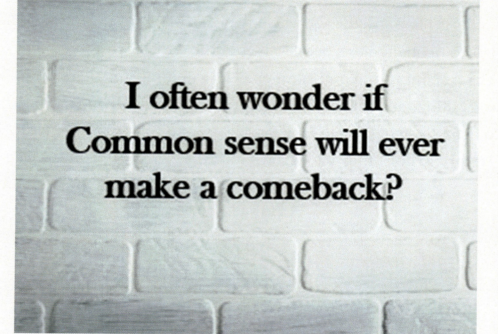

I often wonder if
Common sense will ever
make a comeback?

Obsession
IS A WORD That
Lazy people USE TO
Depict
Dedicated people

~Howard Cole~

Ladies, Chivalry isn't extinct, it just went wherever being lady-like went.

~Howard Cole~

Keep in mind, what you do for yourself is based upon what you think about yourself! "Black people are the only race who take their most valuable belonging, their kids, and solicit their oppressors to teach them and sculpt their brains."

~Howard Cole~

Grown folks get to a specific age where they don't require any drama. They couldn't care less to fight anymore, because if compelled to, they will not fight fair. They won't care about your damn emotional state of mind and there are no weapons they won't utilize against you. Its best to simply leave individuals 50 years old and older to their, morning coffee, Cognac, cigars and Apple Cider Vinegar. The moral to this story is, don't fuck with grown folk, they will hurt your fucking feelings.

~Howard Cole~

Don't lose shit you love. looking at shit you like.

My best friend Chris shared a joke with me,
I chuckled until tears streamed down my face. He shared the exact same joke again and I chuckled, yet not as hard. He repeatedly told me the same joke so many times I quit chuckling. He said, "If you can't continue to chuckle at the same joke again and again, why do you continue shedding tears over individuals who hurt you again and again?

~Howard Cole~

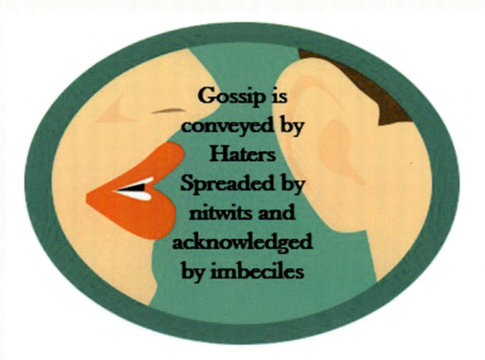

Gossip is conveyed by Haters Spreaded by nitwits and acknowledged by imbeciles

Quit calling motherfucka's who don't call you. Quit visiting motherfucka's who don't know where you live. Quit setting aside time for motherfucka's who don't have energy for you. Quit spending money on motherfucka's who don't spend money on you. Quit considering motherfucka's who don't consider you. You will make yourself emotionally bankrupt. You can love somebody from afar and I'm not just talking about romantic relationships but all relationships; friends, family, boyfriends and girlfriends. Treat motherfucka's the way they treat you and stop over extending yourself and giving affection where it's not returned. Life is sufficiently troublesome without asking people for their affection and consideration. The least you can do for yourself is to involve yourself with individuals who really love and care about you. Involve yourself with individuals that don't consider you to be an alternative. There's nothing worse than wasting time on individuals who treat you like you are replaceable.

~Howard Cole~

The coolest individuals I've at any point met in my life have the most beautiful past, they've led lives of danger, settled on terrible decisions, experienced life lessons, traveled, and they're not scared of being genuine. Worn out embroidered works of art woven of comparable strings, they're my type of individuals. My most loved shades of insanity.

~Howard Cole~

Every now and then I have thoughts of giving up, then I remind myself, I have a bunch of motherfuckers to prove wrong.

~Howard Cole~

Don't Criticize a clown for performing like a clown, question yourself why you keep going to the Circus.

Avoid "STILL" people!! Still BROKE, Still BORROWING, Still whining about the same circumstances, Still HATIN, Still pursuing the SAME man/woman, Still INSECURE, Still IMMATURE, Still INSINCERE, Still DECEIVING, Still STUCK ON STUPID, Still AINT GON CHANGE, still (and always will be) A PAIN IN THE ASS!!

~Howard Cole~

Cream & Sugar Please.

(The lighter side)

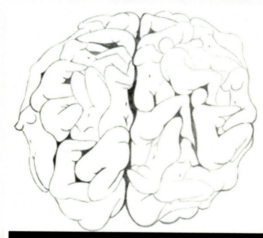

"The Male Brain In Their Teens, 20's, 30's, 40's & 50's"

You should always commit 100% at work...
20% Monday
40% Tuesday
23% Wednesday
12% Thursday
5% Friday

My patience for imbeciles is very low these days.

I used to have some resistance built up,

But clearly,

There is a different type of strain out there these days!

~Howard Cole~

I 'm a product of a

Wooden Spoon

Lead Paint

No Car Seat

No Bike Helmet

Back of A Pickup Truck Riding

Water Hose Drinking

---Survivor ---

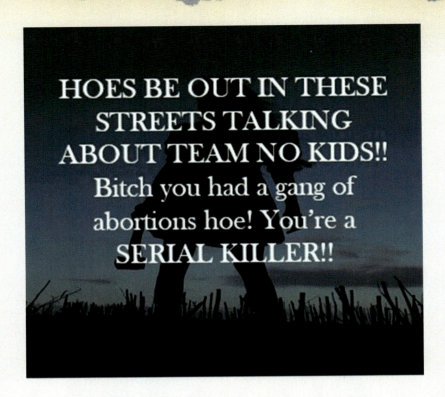

HOES BE OUT IN THESE STREETS TALKING ABOUT TEAM NO KIDS!! Bitch you had a gang of abortions hoe! You're a SERIAL KILLER!!

You ever observe your kid do some dumb shit, and you contemplate to yourself "you get that stupid ass shit from your momma side of the family"

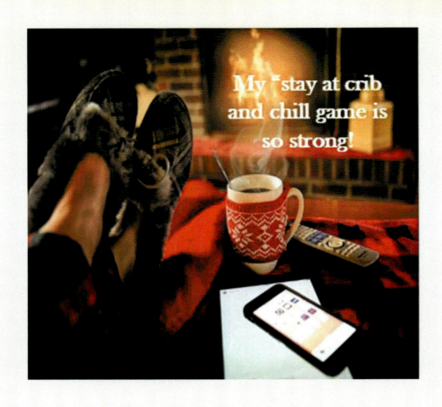

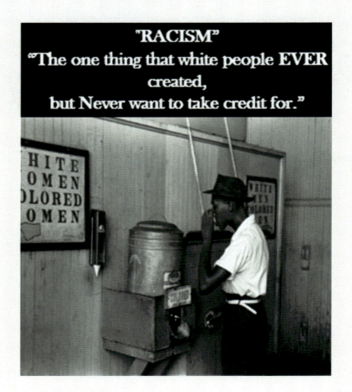

MY WIFE CAUGHT ME BLOW DRYING MY PENIS THIS EVENING AND ASKED ME WHAT I WAS DOING. OBVIOUSLY "WARMING UP YOUR DINNER" WASN'T THE CORRECT RESPONSE.

The shit you find when you clean under your bed after quite some time.

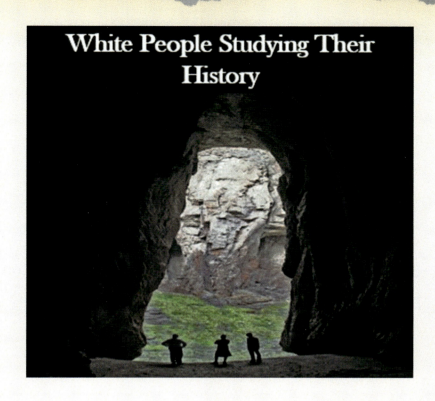

White People Studying Their History

Son: Pops, I want to get hitched
Pops: Okay, Apologize to me.
Son: Why?
Pops: Apologize to me.
Son: Why? I didn't do anything?
Pops: Just Apologize.
Son: Why... what have I done wrong?
Pops: Apologize son.
Son: For What???
Pops: Apologize!
Son: Please, just tell me what for?!
Pops: Apologize...
Son: Ok, Pops... I apologize.
Pops: There! You've finished training. When you learn to apologize for no reason at all, then you're ready to get hitched!

Anticipating results from an election is like anticipating your grade on a class project.
You know you did your shit correct, but you scared everybody else fucked it up.

~Howard Cole~

Dear God,
A few months ago, you took my favorite singer Aretha Franklin. The
next month, you took my favorite actor; Burt Reynolds. This month,
you took another one of my favorite singers; Nancy Wilson.
I just want to let you know that my favorite President is Donald Trump.
Yours sincerely,

~Howard Cole~

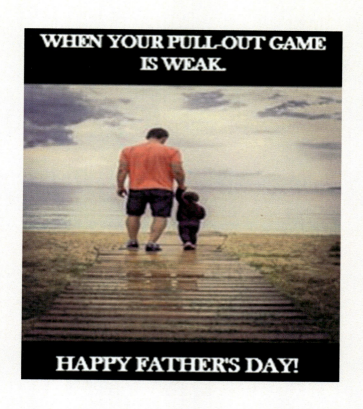

Laughter is the soul's medicine

Teacher: Rontai, how old is your father?

Rontai: He is 6 years

Teacher: What? How is this possible

Rontai: He became my father only when I was born.

(kids are always quick to speak their minds.)

Teacher: Shonta` go to the map and find North America.

Shontà: Here it is.

Teacher: Correct. Now, class, who discovered America

Class: Shonta`

Teacher: Dontai, how do spell 'crocodile?'

Dontai: K-R-O-K-O-D-I-A-L

Teacher: No, that's wrong

Dontai: Maybe it is wrong, but you asked me how I spell it.

Teacher: Chris, what is the chemical formula for water?

Chris: H I J K L M N O

Teacher: What are you talking about?

Chris: Yesterday you said it's H to O.

Teacher: Val, your composition on 'My Dog' is the
same as your brother's. Did you copy his?

Val: No, sir; It's the same dog.

Teacher: Kwante`, what do call a person who keeps on
talking when people are no longer interested?

Kwante`: A teacher.

The Last Drop

My LITTLE son THAT's named after ME (Poem)
Dedicated to my son Howard Lee Cole III

A careful man, I want to be;
For my little son named after me.
I never risk going astray,
For fear my son will go the exact same way.

I cannot once escape his eyes;
Whatever my son sees pops do, he tries.
Just like me, he says he's expiring to be,
My little son named after me.

My son believes I'm nice and fine,
My son believes in every word of mine.
The evil in me, he must not see;
My little son named after me.

I must keep in mind, as I go
Through summer's sun and winter's snow,
I'm building for the years to be,
For my little son named after me.

~Howard Cole~

Acknowledgements

Shontà` Jones Cole

Howard Lee Cole III

Dontai Cole

Rontai Cole

Walter Cole

Sandra Cole

Juanita Irving

Anthony Cole

Juanita Jefferson

Chris Jefferson

Val James

Kwante Hampton

Mike Thompson

Tina Divina

Mark Moses

Jennifer Mauceri

Forrest Barnes

Chanel P. Landreaux

Jack Davis

Johneisha Patrinakos

Porsha Irving

Stephan Johnson

Brenda "Sanchez: Johnson

Family, Friends and Relatives